Long Live the King

soulation PRESS

To Rachel Wolf

Long Live the King
Copyright © 2013 by Dale Fincher & Jonalyn Fincher
www.soulation.org

Published by Soulation Press

Soulation
PO Box 772574
Steamboat Springs, CO 80477

Cover & Interior design by
Jeff Gifford Creative
www.jeffgiffordcreative.com

Cover & Interior photos by
iStockPhoto.com

ISBN: 978-0-9885606-1-1

Printed in the United States of America

soulation PRESS

TABLE
of
CONTENTS

INTRODUCTION

We prepare for times that are significant for us. We buy new clothes or reserve a table at a good restaurant. We remember our first Easter clothes, the first times we attended Good Friday services and Sunday morning Resurrection celebrations.

Jesus also prepared himself for his death and resurrection by spending time with those closest to him, teaching about the things that mattered to him, and clinging to the Father as his final week crescendoed into horrible pain.

We at Soulation want to help you change the way you prepare for Easter's sunrise of hope. Open these pages to find meditations following Jesus' footsteps as he neared the cross.

Easter week is also called Passion week. The Greek meaning behind "passion" is "suffering." Yet passion is also known as a strong emotion toward an object, often in a loving way. We welcome you to intentionally prepare for both love and suffering.

Our week begins with Jesus in the temple courts. On Monday, Jesus confronts people who hijacked spirituality and subjected it to their own design. On Tuesday, Jesus reveals who will join and who will reject the kingdom of God. The Gospel writers give Thursday particular attention, so we'll spend Wednesday and Thursday noticing Jesus movements. We'll meditate on the moments when he washes his disciples' feet, exhibiting the humble love and community that he wants to define their lives. Thursday evening the disciples learn the hard road of prayer in the darkness of the Garden of Gethsemane. Friday is a heavy reading day as we saturate our imaginations in the suffering and death of the Messiah, his darkest hour and ours. For the weekend, Saturday, offering a poem to fill the Sabbath morning, followed by reflections on rest. Sunday finds Jesus walking out of the grave and appearing to several women, who begin sharing the world-stopping news. The dead King is alive again.

Easter is about noticing that God didn't botch things up when he made humans. Jesus' resurrection means humans are pretty fine stuff, fine enough to love, fine enough to battle against the shadows of the cemeteries, and fine enough to forever share his creativity with forever. His resurrection means that, in sharing his life, he promises we ultimately have nothing to fear, nothing to hide, and nothing to lose.

Be ready to watch your heart open and your mind expand as you read winsome apologetics and accessible spiritual formation centered on Jesus' sacrifice and resurrection. This Easter let's learn how to become more fully human, like our Savior who bore our sins so we might become more ourselves.

Sharing in the light and life of the empty tomb,

Dale and Jonalyn Fincher

How to Read this Book

You will not find trite or used-up words in these pages. Therefore, we recommend intentional space between readings.

If you like reading in small doses, you may prefer to choose just one reading per day. Reading more or less does not make you more or less spiritual. If you skip a day, just start on the new day and keep going. You will find treasures on every page you read.

The goal is to meditate on Jesus' last week. Each day we've included the passages from Scripture that correspond to our essays. You might use the Scripture to familiarize yourself with Jesus' movements, miracles, and sermons before you read our meditations. Reading Scripture will enhance your experience, but reading these passages is not required to understand our reflections. Regardless, this reader will make you aware of Jesus' final week and what his words and actions mean.

Each day we include two articles (except Friday). We recommend dividing these articles with time. For example: you could read one each morning at breakfast and the other in the evening before bed. Or if you have little ones who don't leave time for reading, enjoy one before your feet hit the ground in the morning and read the other during the kids' nap time to soften and alter the work that typically fills your days.

On Friday, we've provided specific instructions for accompanying Jesus at four stopping points on his way to the cross. You can read all four or just one on Good Friday.

On Saturday, we've given instruction on how to space those reflections on Sabbath.

We've also included links to bonus audio and video. While these will enhance the feelings and thoughts of each day, feel free to substitute these talks for a reading when you need a break from the written word. Or you can return to these talks later when you want a summary of the teachings from *Long Live The King*.

And if you have come across this reader without Easter appearing soon on the calendar, read at your leisure to see how the King of the Jews died and lived again during his most remarkable week.

MONDAY

May you never place walls between
the light and yourself.

John O'Donohue
Irish priest and poet

With palm leaves in his hair and the praise of the
multitude in his ears, Jesus enters the temple courts.

He drives out all who hijacked spirituality to make it fit
their design and profit.

In the vacuum of power, he sits and makes room to
heal the blind and lame people while children shout,
"Hosanna to the Son of David!"

Matthew 21

Boutique Spirituality
By Jonalyn Fincher

When we moved to Steamboat Springs, Colorado, I met a high concentration of people who saw the world as their playground. These mountain-loving, ranch-owning, ski-hungry types were similar in their spiritual taste. The people who populate small Colorado towns are drawn to customized forms of religion. It's not just Colorado types, people all over America are increasingly drawn to designing their own religion. I have a name for this new practice: boutique spirituality.

The point of a boutique is to buy what suits you, your home, your decorating style. Boutiques are usually one-of-a-kind places to shop, so you can get the fashion you want without combing through piles of cookie-cutter clothes. Religion is quickly turning into a boutique shop, where we create our spirituality to fit us, rather than expecting God to change us.

> Religion is quickly turning into a boutique shop

One bumper sticker illustrates boutique religion perfectly. Across bumpers in America I've seen the sticker: "COEXIST," where every letter holds a symbol of a religion. The "C" is an Islamic crescent and star, the "X" is a Star of David, the "I" is dotted with the yin and yang, and the "T" is a Christian cross. Basically, the bumper sticker teaches, "You choose what works for you. Just live at peace with all those around you." But by laying each symbol side-by-side, the bumper sticker makes an additional secular commentary: it assumes all religions to be essentially equal. Each one gives us an option, but no spiritual path offers more or better truth than any other. The coexist bumper sticker treats religion like an accessory. Choosing a spirituality becomes as innocuous as choosing a decorating style. Find one that works with your life. I like vintage, you like modern. You follow Buddha's teachings, I follow Jesus', and we could even blend the two. Some people like several spiritual guides at once (The *Life of Pi* comes to mind). We both leave the spiritual boutique with things that suit our taste. In the same way, boutique religion gives us a way to feel spiritual without changing our lives too much.

We have traded the timeless question, "Do we fit God's world?" for a new one, "Does God fit ours?"

In one way I agree with the coexist bumper sticker. Scripture makes it clear that human beings with different beliefs should coexist. Love requires it. The Bible says each person should decide about Jesus Christ according to their own conscience.[1] God teaches us that all human beings are valuable.[2]

But not all these religions believe in freedom of conscience. Even worse, most religions, for most of history, have not valued those who are weak, infirm, female, poor, or elderly. So while believers of different religions can coexist together, their beliefs cannot.

> So while believers of different religions can coexist together, their beliefs cannot.

This is why Buddha left Hinduism, he did not agree with the Hindu practice of mortification of the body. You could even argue that every new religion, from Islam to Rastafarianism, builds upon and departs from previous religious beliefs.

[1] *2 Corinthians 4:1-2*
[2] *Genesis 1:27*   13

Every religion offers different answers to what is wrong with the world, what is wrong with humans, and how to fix the problems.

Take the Christian belief that God is a personal judge who will make all wrongs right at the end of the world. Compare this with Buddhism. The Buddha taught that there is no personal judge, no all-powerful being that fixes injustice.

Either a judge lives to work out justice or he does not. Which is it for you? You cannot put both into your shopping cart because they contradict each other, like warm ice. As soon as you choose one, the other gets excluded by definition. Either God is personal and all-powerful and transcends us, as in Christianity, or there is no personal God and we work out our injustice through knowledge, meditation, and working off bad karma, as in Buddhism's Middle Way.

While you can love those who practice the Middle Way, you can serve them and even die for them as Jesus did, you cannot believe in both an impersonal universe and a personal Judge.

Even with boutique spirituality, we have a choice to make. Surprising to me, in the final Monday of Jesus' life, he made it clear what he believed. He was controversial even though he knew it wasn't safe. Jesus taught that a personal Judge lived who he called Father. And Jesus acted like his Father's judgments trumped the spiritual climate of his day.

When Jesus strode into the Temple he made a bold move that flies in the face of the coexist bumper sticker.

Jesus was about to call out the way religious people (like those who sold sacrificial animals for the Temple) could use religious places (like the Temple) to plot and take advantage of those who simply wanted to obey God. Jesus was incensed that these spiritually abusive leaders were warming their hands by God's sacrificial fires.[3]

When Jesus forcibly drove out the money-changers, he was acting as if his beliefs about God could not coexist with the spiritual leaders, who he called "robbers in a den."

In this first day of his Passion week, Jesus teaches that some beliefs are so harmful they must be driven out, along with the people who use God's name to shelter their abuse. That challenge is upon us today. Where do we start? What beliefs do we tolerate and which do we drive out?

> Jesus teaches that some beliefs are so harmful they must be driven out.

Aren't false beliefs all around us? How can we simply drive all these people out?

I suggest we begin within the church, just as Jesus began within the Jewish temple. Rather than be the first to condemn the gay couple or the pro-choice feminist, let us be sternest with our own, starting with ourselves.

What beliefs are being nurtured within the body of Christ that turn Christians into agents of the Evil One? What beliefs do we nurture that lead us to steal, kill, and destroy? What are Christians reading and writing that cheapen the way we look at men or women, children, or the elderly? How are we allowing Christian communities

Some ideas are not worthy of us or our humanity that Jesus died to save.

to harbor those who abuse others? There are beliefs we cannot allow to coexist with our love for Jesus. For some ideas are not worthy of us or our humanity that Jesus died to save.

Healing the Blind
By Jonalyn Fincher

A good friend of mine decided to pursue yoga, not merely for the stretching, but because the meditation allowed her to clear her mind. A friend from college decided that in order to build up his positive energy, he must feng shui his house. My pharmacist left the church he used to attend and lent me a CD on channeling.

Have you ever heard a friend say, "I'm spiritual but not religious"? Yet these friends, for all their anti-religion, are often quite dogmatic about what is the "proper" way to be spiritual. I've even had several try to convert me, to sell me on the healing power of quinoa and the energy of jade jewelry. How do I talk to people about a real God when they believe spirituality is something they can design and invent?

Just as Jesus cleared a path for the marginalized (in his day it was the lame and blind) to enter the Temple courts without fear, so we can clear a path for those who would be unwelcome in most small groups. We can help those who are searching for spiritual truth and healing by becoming safe and kind ambassadors for the Great Physician.

Here are a few tips to ponder and consider:[4]

1. Respect each other as valuable humans
Regardless of what someone else believes, no matter how unreasonable it sounds, we must treat them with

[4]These tips and more can be found in *Coffee Shop Conversations: Making the Most of Spiritual Small Talk* by Dale Fincher and Jonalyn Fincher.

respect. As far as I can tell, Jesus never interrogated those who wanted healing except with one sentence, "What do you want me to do for you?" For example, each Wiccan, Taoist, Buddhist is valuable because each is human; it's only their ideas that are different. Even if they are trying to run as fast as they can away from Christianity, treat them with the highest value that Jesus offers: every person bears the image of God. Treating them this way opens doors for respectful, authentic conversation.

Each Wiccan, Taoist, Buddhist is valuable because each is human.

Respect and gentleness are the fertile soil of relationship and love. We may need to invest in someone else's life over the long haul. I have a friend I've made at the local coffee shop. I've given her a book to read after I found out her history of sexual abuse. We've spoken over a dozen times since and only once did I bring up the book. As soon as I did, I could see she felt guilty that she hadn't read it. Patience is a better apologetic for her soul than a push to read the book I gave. That's the kind of respect I want from my friends—long and steady patience.

Listen with love and remain un-shockable.

2. Step into their shoes
Ask questions to understand what attracts them to their designer spirituality. You may ask, "How does meditation help you in your life?" Then, be an excellent listener. This is important for all relationships. Listen with love and remain un-shockable even if you disagree with what they say.

They might say, "I feel so much better when I'm done, like my body is cleansed, like my mind is lighter." Listen, nod, (even smile!), let them know you understand what they mean. This is what active listening means. Take this chance to really understand another worldview. It's a great gift they're giving to you. Be careful not to jump on their ideas. That will not foster trust. You want to get into their shoes for the sake of understanding them, not for the sake of tricking them into being vulnerable so you can accuse or contradict them. When they give their answers, take mental notes.

Wrestle with their ideas on your own. Learn to decipher what is true about their ideas from what isn't. Are there any connecting points? Even opposing worldviews can find truth to agree upon. Think about the possible contradictions or ramifications of their ideas. Watch their back from the danger of bad ideas (just as you would want them to return the favor). Analyze their motivation and see if their spiritual practices actually deliver what they are looking for. How helpful are their views? This will be good material to use later when the conversation naturally comes up again. You can say, "You know, I was thinking about what you said the other day, and I was puzzled about how meditating makes you feel loved. Can you help me see it more clearly?" Let them explain it more, and here you can interject and voice what doesn't make sense.

3. Talk about God's personality
When Jesus was in Jerusalem, loved by the crowds but despised by the religious leaders, he made a challenging statement, "Truly I say to you that the tax collectors and prostitutes will get into the kingdom of God before you."[5]

---

[5]*Matthew 21:31*

We may believe many of our friends are far from the kingdom of God because they don't go to church or talk about God, but they may be close to the Kingdom of God much more like the tax collectors and prostitutes of Jesus' day. It's easy to assume that some types of people are not near to God.

God's kingdom is closer to the humble, the seekers of truth, the hungry souls, the poor in spirit, than the self-assured religious leaders. Jesus' final days teach us this.

In this post-Christian culture much of our work in discipling souls to know Jesus is connecting dots. Most people believe in God. They just don't realize the God they pray to has already reached down to connect and heal them.

The God they pray to has already reached down to connect and heal them.

Here's one way to connect the dots. We start with the assumption that most people have: God is loving. We can use that assumption to show them that God is a person.

Ask your friend if they pray to God. Most people do, even if they pray to a life force, or energy, or the Goddess. Find out what words they use to talk about their Higher Power.

If your friend prays, you can ask something like this: "Does the Goddess (choose the appropriate word they use for their God) love you?" You may want to give examples: "Have you experienced your Higher Power interacting with you? Does the Goddess have feelings? Do you think the Goddess chooses?" Or you can refer to their prayer experiences, "Does the Goddess hear and answer your prayers?"

If their God hears them and loves them and answers their prayers (as much as the spiritual designer says God or the Goddess does), then this is a God who reveals himself to those he loves. Now you can ask, "If the Goddess is loving, how does she reveal herself to you?"

Love reveals. Love wants to be known. If God is love, he is a person. Only persons can love. And he is a God who wants to be known. He doesn't want to be invented anymore than we want our lovers to invent us.

> He doesn't want to be invented anymore than we want our lovers to invent us.

As you dialogue, listen closely. Try not to be discouraged when your friends still don't want to hear about Jesus. Jesus' PR has been damaged for listeners today. It will take time to rebuild Jesus as he was in Scripture. The same Jesus who turned the moneychangers' tables upside down in the Temple took time to rebuild the God of Israel's reputation through parables and questions. Not all is changed in one conversation.

> It will take time to rebuild Jesus as he was in Scripture.

Our friends have to work through their beliefs, and it's best when they have a loving friend at their side. Remember we are also easily blinded. None of us is so enlightened by Jesus' truth that we have all true beliefs. We all have poor places in our spirit, and we are all at risk of becoming assured that we should always play the spiritual teacher. By extending care with humility, risk, and love, we invite one another up the winding road home where our Father welcomes those who seek him in spirit and in truth.[6]

[6]John 4:23

TUESDAY

What is man that You take thought of him,
And the son of man that You care for him?
Yet You have made him a little lower than God,
And You crown him with glory and majesty!

David
Jewish king, shepherd, poet

Jesus spent two days in the temple courts where he
weaves some of the clearest parables of
the kingdom of God and the end times:

the ten virgins and their oil,
the landowner and his slaves,
the master and his vineyard.

Jesus reminds the Jewish people what God's kingdom
is really like: a wedding feast.

He casts eight woes upon the Pharisees and explains why
their crimes are so dire. The Pharisees do not value all
humans as image bearers of God: the thirsty, the sick,
the poor, the naked, and the imprisoned.

The Pharisees do not know the God of Israel and one day
he will not know them.

Matthew 21, 23-24

Unworthy, Not Worthless
By Dale Fincher

In a recent publication that arrived in our mail, I read about a modern worship experience in church. One of the worship leaders interviewed said the purpose of worship is to remember that we are worms before God.

That we are worms.

Is that the good news story?

Jesus clearly exposed the Pharisees for loving honor rather than serving others.[7] Pride is obviously an abomination to God, but making ourselves lower than dirt is not the way to be a servant. We must begin with what God thinks of us, neither higher than others, nor lower than others. We are of earth, fashioned from the ground, but with God's breath within us. It strikes me as helpful to note how the Latin root for earth is "humus," also the root word for humility. Our earthly origins link both our origins and the virtue Jesus talked so much about. "The greatest among you shall be your servant."[8]

> Making ourselves lower than dirt is not the way to be a servant.

But servants do not think of themselves as worms. In the critically acclaimed and moving movie, *Life is Beautiful*, Guido learns from his uncle, Eliseo, that a servant is one who is like God. "Think of a sunflower, they bow to the sun. But if you see some that are bowed too far down, it means they're dead. You're here serving… Serving is the

[7]*Matthew 23:1-12*
[8]*Matthew 23:11*

supreme art. God is the first of servants. God serves men but he's not a servant to men."

My hunch is that we've lost the virtue of humility precisely because we've confused two very important words and made them one.

Unworthy. Worthless.

These do not mean the same thing. But when we attach them to each other, we end up talking and believing that our unworthiness means our worthlessness. In Jesus' parables the Pharisees also conflated these words. They devoured widow's finances, shunned those who didn't look like leaders, ignored the sick, the hungry, the prisoners.[9] They thought these people were unworthy and therefore worthless.

A teen told me how worthless he felt. "I'm a sinner, I'm worthless," he said. To be a sinner meant to be worthless. He tied the two together, thinking that a wrong choice in his past made his soul valueless. He was living like the Pharisees taught others to live.

"No," I replied, "you are not worthless. Being a sinner cannot ever make you worthless."

> Being a sinner cannot ever make you worthless.

Most of his church life, this teen heard that being a sinner makes you undeserving of friendship with God, unworthy of inheriting God's promises of peace and joy and life everlasting. Sinning or missing the mark does make us unworthy to live in friendship with God. But somehow he made the small step that unworthy meant worthless.

"Unworthy" is failing to live up to requirements. If you cheat your employer, you do not deserve a raise. If you fail to study for a test, you do not deserve a high grade. If you forget your child's birthday, you do not deserve a happy child.

> "Unworthy" is failing to live up to requirements.

You are unworthy of reward when you fail to do what is reward-worthy. You cannot be worthy of winning the Boston Marathon if you come in last. You do not deserve God's rewards of peace and joy when, through sin, you've done nothing to deserve these rewards.

That is what it means to be unworthy. Your merits fall short. You are unworthy to be honored for winning the race.[10]

To be worthless, however, is quite different. While being unworthy is about deserving merits, being worthless is about our value. If you lost the Boston Marathon, you are as full of value as the person who won. If you forgot your child's birthday, you are no less valuable than the parent who remembered weeks in advance and rented a bounce house for the occasion.

The distance between unworthy merit and worthless value is the distance between east and west.

Jesus did not come for the worthless. He came for the unworthy. He talked about the poor and sick, the widows and children, the naked and hungry, because he knew everyone would see that those types were unworthy. What tweaked the Pharisees so badly is that unworthy people had worth to God. It confused them and it confuses us.

[10]Romans 4:4

If we cannot earn love, then we refuse it. Isn't that the common struggle we all face? We wrongly believe undeserved love is a type of condescension for others to be superior. But Jesus says that something about us, even in our sin, has worth and he reaches down to pull us up.

Jesus came for those who are valuable. His coming did not make us valuable.

You are human after all. Humans cannot give themselves value. Humans were made valuable from the start, without our consultation, whether we liked it or not.[11] A popular Christian writer once criticized me for this idea, insisting that Jesus made us valuable on the cross. "It's modern people who are concerned about value because we're too obsessed with economics," he wrote.

But as I read Scripture, I find a God who affirms our value from the day of our birth. When God created humans he made us valuable in Eden before any temptation to think otherwise, calling his creation "good," which is a value statement. And God makes a plan to rescue us as soon as we fall, even before the Law and Sacrifices.[12]

> I find a God who affirms our value from the day of our birth.

Perhaps David was having a wormy, low day when he wrote Psalm 8, but he affirms man's value still, even before the sacrifice of Jesus:

> When I consider Your heavens, the work of Your fingers,
> The moon and the stars, which You have ordained;
> What is man that You take thought of him,
> And the son of man that You care for him?

[11]Genesis 1:27
[12]Genesis 3:15

Yet You have made him a little lower than God,
And You crown him with glory and majesty!
You make him to rule over the works of Your hands;
You have put all things under his feet.[13]

Jesus said, "What does it profit a man to gain the world and lose his soul?" Jesus doesn't avoid even economic metaphors to show us our value.[14] Our value is worth more than all our merits, worth more than all the world.

Our value is worth more than all our merits, worth more than all the world.

Does God then reach down to us because we've done good deeds, obligating God to pay attention to us? No. We cannot obligate God to us through anything we do.

Does God reach down to us because he loves the valuable humans he has made, obligating himself to what he has made? Absolutely.

Jesus' forgiveness does not make us suddenly valuable either, as if a worm collection was suddenly wanted. No, Jesus' forgiveness makes us deserving of the reward of knowing God. His forgiveness pulls a human soul out of the mire, just like a good mechanic can pull a classic car wreck from the dump to rebuild the engine and make it growl again. This is what the Scripture means by grace. Jesus' forgiveness reminds us, again and again, that we are valuable, though our merits are short.

Let me say it again, though it may sound unusual to some ears: we can never obligate God to save us. But he obligated himself through love to save his valuable creation. This obligation to value the least human being

[13]*Psalms 8:3-6*
[14]*Mark 8:36*

is a requirement he puts upon all his followers. "The King will answer and say to them, 'Truly I say to you, to the extent that you did it to one of these brothers of Mine, even the least of them, you did it to Me.' "[15]

> This obligation to value the least human being is a requirement he puts upon all his followers.

We are unworthy, but not worthless. By facing the cross, Jesus demonstrated we are worthwhile and loved, no matter what we do.[16] God loves the valuable and teaches us how to see one another beyond what we deserve. That's why Jesus lived and died.

[15]*Matthew 25:40*
[16]*Romans 5:8*

Tracking the Source
By Dale Fincher

We huddled into a small, crowded room in Monument, Colorado, fifteen of us resting in disjointed rows of seats to hear the music of Andrew Peterson.

I discovered Andrew in the late 1990s. His name came up in a music store as I shared with the owner how much I missed Rich Mullins. The owner handed me Andrew's first CD. And I immediately found a kindred spirit.

I play many of Andrew's songs on the guitar, melodies I make in my living room to the audience of a lamp, a coffee table, and a corgi or two.

My chance to meet Andrew finally came at a small house-concert where a few of us gathered around to hear our favorites. He opened with Rich Mullins' song, "Hello, Old Friends," which spilled happy memories into my soul.

As I quietly sang along to most of the songs that evening, I reminded myself this wasn't another playlist on the iPod. This was live. Five feet from me, the songs that stirred my heart were spilling out of the heart that made them. I had tracked the songs to their source.

> The songs that stirred my heart were spilling out of the heart that made them.

That's one of those strange sensations we have in life, when someone who is far comes near. It is a universal feeling, validated by the amount of money people throw at gossip magazines, like *People*, just to get a little closer to the celebrities they have come to love on the silver screen.

I've had similar feelings with famous objects too. In fourth grade, we learned of the Rosetta Stone. I remember the picture of that stone, and I remember when my mother took me to the British Museum later that year to see it on display. A throng of visitors surrounded it, but I still managed to stretch my eleven-year-old hand to touch it with my fingers. Except for a couple of mummies, I don't remember paying much attention to anything else in the museum on that visit. But I do recall returning home and telling my classmates, "You know that picture in our history book of the Rosetta Stone? Well, I touched it!"

I have felt similar things in visiting the Vatican, the Liberty Bell, Mount Rushmore, the Roman Forum, the Isle of Delphi, and the Wittenberg door where Martin Luther nailed his *Ninety-Five Theses*. I replayed what I knew from books about those places. But at the source, everything came to life. I walked the same cobbled stones, entered the same architecture, and looked up at the same sky as the most famous people of antiquity. "Here is where it began," I thought, "where this ordinary place came to life."

I can imagine that when the day comes that I get to visit Israel, I will find myself even more amazed. I want to sit by Jacob's well and recite the scene where Jesus offered living water to a Samaritan woman. I want to see the battlefield where the giant fell. One day I hope to stand spellbound on Golgotha and look at the place where God answered the problem of evil in the wounds of the Man from Galilee. I will mouth the words still hanging in the air, "Father, forgive them, for they do not know what they are doing."[17]

[17] *Luke 23:34*

I will have tracked the story to its source. The tracking takes preparation and the inconvenience of a trip. I imagine my mother's plans to cart an eleven and eight year old with her to the British Museum. It's so easy to justify not going. "They won't really remember it. It's so expensive and time-consuming."

I will have tracked the story to its source.

Tracking the source means we inconvenience ourselves to hunt for it.

Tracking the source means we inconvenience ourselves to hunt for it. We must prepare, like the five virgins who were waiting and ready for the bridegroom, expecting to see, ready even at midnight.[18]

As I ponder this, I think how all things are tracked to a single Source. The laugh of a friend, the moon's shadows, the waving of leaves in an autumn breeze, the suckling of a child at a mother's breast, the love on a honeymoon, the crescendo at the opera house, and the gentleness of sharing your abundance with one in need. All of these, too, have their source in one unifying Person.

When the gates of heaven are parted wide to bring in all friends of God, I know when we turn toward the Throne we will see a familiar face. It will be familiar, not because we have seen it before, but because in it, we will see all the things we have loved for so long. In him we will understand the source of joy, laughter, promise, grace, love, and life itself. We will long to serve this Servant of all.

We will have tracked all good things back to their source in God himself.

We will have tracked all good things back to their source in God himself.

[18]Matt 25:1-13

And when we are with him, we will know that all the stirrings of beauty, truth, and goodness we found in musicians and museums were mere echoes, spilled from a bountiful place we will one day call home.

WEDNESDAY

I love thee to the depth and breadth
and height my soul can reach.

Elizabeth Barrett Browning
British poet

Halfway through the week we begin to see Jesus
intentionally humble himself with his disciples.

Tomorrow we will spend special time on Jesus' final
prayers, so today we fast-forward a little bit.

What does Jesus do during his final meal to enjoy his
closest friends? He blesses them

by washing their feet,
by sharing food and wine,
and by praying for them.

John 13-17

Greatness of Soul
By Jonalyn Fincher

Once on a flight from London to Chicago, my husband enjoyed a movie while I cared for our restless son. Later, we found out he was suffering from two ear infections on top of a stomach bug.

As long as I nursed him, my son was mostly calm. But he would stop every few minutes to cry. I was anxious that the stomach bug would appear *en force*, so I curtailed feeding him whenever I could. The strategy made me unhappy and my son more-so. My husband, not knowing my son's struggle as much as I did, advised, "Keep nursing."

I reluctantly agreed, but was thinking, *So you can keep watching your movie? Must be really nice.*

Deep down I felt my sacrifice for my son signaled my superiority as a parent. I was willing (sort of) to give up the movie to ensure my son was okay.

Most of my sacrifice was a threadbare cloak unable to cover the dark-hearted resentment I bore toward my husband. Add a holier-than-thou attitude which I nursed as I nursed my son.

So when my son decided he'd had enough and emptied his stomach all over the seat and aisle, you might imagine I had plenty of choice words for my husband's strategy of "just keep

> I felt vindicated and yet the words I used didn't make me feel any better.

nursing." I felt vindicated and yet the words I used didn't make me feel any better.

Pride loomed.

What is pride? A cousin to selfishness, a sister to envy, and a twin of conceit, it is described in Scripture as lofty eyes, vaulting oneself, boastful pride of life, thinking ourselves more important than others. Prideful people are self-absorbed (or narcissistic) and conceited. They think often about and much of themselves.

Pride is inherently comparative. Pride says I deserve more than you or you or you. Pride often funds other sins because we believe something about ourselves is better than yours: our beautiful or interesting, quirky or authentic, athletic or sophisticated edge makes us more valuable. Then we sneer, purse our lips in distaste, or expect ourselves to be singled out for honor and admiration.

> Pride often funds other sins.

When my first book didn't make big sales, I was shocked. How could my ideas not resonate above others on spirituality and womanhood?

Above others.

This expectation that my ideas deserved more than another was pride. The same was at work when I wanted to prove my husband's parenting strategy on a trans-Atlantic flight was substandard to mine.

C.S. Lewis writes that our Enemy bends us to become

aware of our humility, which has the diabolical purpose of twisting our humility into comparison. I'm more humble than you are.

And yet, humility is not identical to naïveté. Humility is not ignoring our strengths or forgetting the way our soul shines with gifts. Jesus could not humble himself to wash his disciples' feet unless he knew how to serve them.

Humility begins with steady confidence in the gifts God has given us. Humble people know the space they occupy and how they can use that to serve. Jesus could wrap a towel around his waist and wash his disciples' feet because he knew who he was. No one, not even a Roman crucifixion team, could rob him of the greatness in his soul.

> Humility begins with steady confidence in the gifts God has given us.

Humility is about how we approach our power and weakness. It's about refusing to assert our will as preeminent over others. Humble people use their greatness to make great things for others. And when wronged, a humble person doesn't expect groveling before they make up.

Jesus washed the feet of the man who he knew would betray him. How must he have felt as he dried the soles of Judas' feet knowing those soles would carry him to the Sanhedrin?

Jesus washed the feet of the disciple, Peter, who he knew would deny him publicly in a matter of hours.

Jesus would tell them as they reclined and ate together

that he had overcome the world. This is humility, steadfast confidence in what we can do and who we belong to. No bravado or false meekness.

The servant Jesus and the teacher Jesus mingled one last time together over the last supper, a lingering picture of how humility lives on this earth. And sometimes I get a picture of that in the people God has put in my life.

As a flight attendant brought napkins and I worked on the mess made on the plane flight, I reluctantly let my husband help. In the end, I had to rely on him to quiet and comfort our son. As I worked, my anger subsided. I took time to revisit my anger.

It wasn't so much my husband or my son that was making me livid. It was my pride. I didn't want to inconvenience the other passengers. I was afraid of how I looked and what a poor impression I was making. I did not know the steady confidence of God's provision, to take care of even my reputation and comfort despite the situation.

In the next few hours on the flight, my husband acted as caretaker, helping my son finally sleep without any food. No bravado or false meekness in him as he bent his body to make a cocoon of safety for our baby. I felt my soul unclench as I watched them both fall soundly sleep. Humility had come, robbed me of my anger, and left me with the blanket of gratitude.

I felt my soul unclench.

The Last Supper
By Jonalyn Fincher

Jesus eagerly began his final meal. He'd been looking forward to this Passover for a long time.[19] This meal held thousands of years of significance for him. As a Jew, he knew that the month of Passover was the God-ordained beginning of the year.[20]

Faithful Jews celebrated Passover, or the Feast of Unleavened Bread, only once a year. The feast was a replica of the meal the Israelites enjoyed as their final supper before leaving Egypt.

For thousands of years, Jews would prepare the hurried loaves, made without leaven because the Israelites hadn't had time to let their bread rise. They would choose and kill a young, tender lamb. In Jerusalem, lamb shanks would be roasting and brought to the table to eat along with bitter herbs and unleavened bread. The lamb would remind the Jewish people of how the Israelites slaughtered a lamb to smear its blood on their doorposts as God commanded.[21] A messy idea that notified the Angel of Death to pass over their home and not slaughter their oldest sons during the final plague of Egypt. Life for life, the blood of a lamb to protect the blood of their sons.[22]

God commanded the Israelites to eat in haste as they would be driven from Egypt the next day. This was the Lord's Passover, when the Lord passed over the doors embellished with lamb's blood and passed judgment against the gods of Egypt.[23]

[19]*Luke 22:14-16*
[20]*Exodus 12:2*
[21]*Exodus 12:7*
[22]*Exodus 12*
[23]*Exodus 12:13-14*

Thousands of years layered meaning into the night when Jesus celebrated the Passover feast, joining his final meal upon earth with the Israelites' final meal as slaves.[24]

As Jesus took a portion of the lamb, did he remember how his cousin called him the "Lamb of God who takes away the sins of the world"?[25] The final supper of the final Lamb.

Wine warmed their insides, flat bread and roasted lamb finished its circles around the table. The sun was long set.

The disciples waited to hear what Jesus would say, little knowing the manifesto of love that Jesus would pray over them. Jesus offered up a cup of wine and said, "A new covenant in my blood."[26]

> The disciples waited to hear what Jesus would say…

I would imagine they felt like many of us do on life-changing days, awed and distracted, wide-eyed but ready to problem solve and help. One disciple pointed out two swords after Jesus foretold his death, as if these could protect Jesus from what was to come.[27]

> Jesus' goal was to love his friends until the end.

Jesus' goal was to love his friends until the end.[28] After a meal so pregnant with meaning, he prayed for their protection and unity. He didn't mince words about Peter's denial or Judas' betrayal. In many ways, this meal was Jesus' deathbed soliloquy. His words in John 17 are the courageous words of love for those he will leave. They are the words of a man facing execution but who can also see beyond the cross to joining the Father.

[24]Exodus 12:17
[25]John 1:29, & 35
[26]Luke 22:20

[27]Luke 22:38
[28]John 13:1

39

Jesus prays, "I am coming to you now, but I say these things while I am still in the world, so that they may have the full measure of my joy within them."[29] For the joy set before him, he would endure the cross, despising its shame. He knew what his work would mean, He had come to make his blessings flow, far as the curse is found. He would see it finished.

He had come to make his blessings flow, far as the curse is found.

Fortified with the meal connecting Jesus with the Jewish history of oppression, he would rise and face his oppressors.

[29]John 17:13

THURSDAY

Surely he took up our pain
and bore our suffering,
yet we considered him punished by God,
stricken by him, and afflicted.

Isaiah
Jewish prophet

When the Passover meal ends,
Jesus leads his disciples to Gethsemane,
and, overwhelmed with sorrow,
he turns to his Father in prayer.

Matthew 26

Invitation to Tears
By Jonalyn Fincher

I've walked into places where my prayers seemed to hit a wall and bounce back, reverberating with my own confusion.

To avoid the heavenly silence that greets my own tears, I've sometimes chosen a shortcut: a laundry list of general requests. "Lord, help me get through today and heal Chris and comfort Sal." I don't pray specifically enough to be able to tell if the answers really come back affirmative.

General prayer is so vast you might never know if God answered. Did the Lord help me get through today or my own extra effort and that espresso?

Sometimes we don't petition God specifically because we think, "God already knows everything I need and want, I don't have to tell him." Why get really specific if he can read our minds?

Why get really specific if he can read our minds?

It is true, God can read our minds.
When Jesus prayed in the Garden, the Father knew his mind. The Father knew what Jesus wanted, to refuse the bitter cup of brutalization, to pass by the heaviness of bearing our sin. And yet, Jesus prays specifically.

I think one reason we avoid specific prayer is that we're avoiding the disappointment. We don't want to be low and sad if God says "no." We feel that our sadness is somehow a failure of our faith in God.

But the invitation to tears is as old as Eden. Weeping is part of the food pyramid nourishing our body and soul in this broken world.

When Jesus was at his lowest, Matthew says he fell on his face and prayed, "My Father, if it is possible, let this cup pass from Me; yet not as I will, but as You will."[30] A specific short prayer in Gethsemane that God would answer with so much clarity.

God would answer with so much clarity.

God would say, "No." This cup would not pass. Jesus would drain it. And facing that reality, our Lord wept.

When I hear God turn me down, I find myself taking a belly-flop into grief. My prayer has failed and it's hard for me to not feel like a failure. I feel sort of dumb, I guess, like God is laughing at me.

It's interesting to remember Jesus' prayer life. Jesus didn't get all his prayers granted. We know because he prayed for specific things and sometimes these specific things did not happen. He prayed three times to leave the cup and God did not grant him his request.[31]

But Jesus was not a failure. And God was not laughing.

When we pray for something, even good things, and God refuses, it seems likely God's silence means gravity, presence, and mutual grief. We know God weeps. Jesus did.

[30]*Matthew 26:39*
[31]*Matthew 26:39-44*

The way we enter grief depends in large part on how firmly we believe God is sitting with us in the tears. Can we call upon God to comfort us even when he refuses our request? King David shows us a way by comparing his grief to a weaned child:

> Surely I have composed and quieted my soul;
> Like a weaned child rests against his mother,
> My soul is like a weaned child within me.
> O Israel, hope in the Lord
> From this time forth and forever.[32]

A child who rests on his mother even while he doesn't receive nourishment from her. Jesus resting in conversation with the Father even while he wept at the silence of heaven.

Did Jesus find peace in the Garden? If he did, it wasn't from his sleepy disciples, nor in the sound of his requests bouncing back to him. Rather, he found it in grieving well. Jesus entered his sorrow before his body bore a mark: "My soul is deeply grieved, to the point of death."[33] Jesus used the last moments of quiet to cry, to feel distress, and to invite the Father to help him. From that exhaustion and honesty he rose, blood soaked, to let Judas kiss his cheek.

Out of tears he began making all things new.

[32]*Psalm 131:2-3*
[33]*Matthew 26:38*

The Problem of Prayer
By Dale Fincher

I've gone round and round with God on prayer. I'm baffled how finite people can dare appeal to an infinite God to persuade him.

Persuading the Almighty leaves me restless. Not merely the idea that he bows his omnipotent presence to hear me, but rather, I feel he should already know better. If my neighbor is going bankrupt, God knows my neighbor more than I do, and knew of the bankruptcy before time began. Why does he wait for my petition before making his move? Or would he have acted already, regardless of my prayers?

> Persuading the Almighty leaves me restless.

People write us, "If I pray for God to do something and then it happens, how do I know it wasn't going to happen anyway? Maybe I just prayed at the right time to make it appear that God was doing something!"

I've wondered myself if petitionary prayer is more lucky charm than appeals to God. I've watched friends use prayer to avoid responsibility, like praying God will open doors without lifting a finger to knock. And I cringe when I hear speakers advertise prayer carelessly, like saying, "If you have enough faith, God will always give you what you want." Or punting to answered prayer as the only explanation for some events that could easily be explained in other ways.

I'm most puzzled (and often angered) that God answers lesser prayers without answering more important ones, like when I lost my wallet. I searched for days and asked God to help me find it. When I eventually did, somehow kicked under my bed, I danced like  the woman who found her coin. But as soon as the lost was found, another weight hung on my heart. For years I had been praying for my mother to be healed of cancer. I would gladly swap a wallet for a mother. But God doesn't make prayer-trades.

After speaking at a Christian college on this theme, several students shared concern that I missed the simple solution. "God answers all prayers: a yes, no, or maybe!" they said. But that hardly settles things. When we weep over unanswered prayer, we weep over requests denied. We weep because he told us to ask and we shall receive. But we did not receive. He told us to knock to open the door. Yet no door opened.[34] The one we implore is the one who taught us to ask expectantly. It is like asking for bread and receiving nothing, not even a stone.[35] It's the granting of some requests and not the granting of others that is so painfully mysterious.

It is good for me to sit fully in these puzzles, to press into the heart of God, and humble myself before the mystery of his purposes. Un-granted prayers pang my heart with a deeper fear: that God may be disinterested.

Is God willy-nilly with his work in the world or is he involved in my story, even when it looks like the world is crumbling before me, my family, and my friends?

[34]*Matthew 7:8*
[35]*Matthew 7:9*

The distinguished Christian philosopher, J.P. Moreland, remarked to our graduate class that one of his greatest obstacles to faith was un-granted prayers. Can we still call God good when it appears he's left us hanging?

Jesus sweated blood in his agony of a prayer un-granted. His disciples, full from a big meal, lounged against olive trees, while Jesus poured over the lonely agony that would soon begin. The same lips that said, "Seek and you will find,"[36] are now seeking hope and finding deep pain. The disciples snoring behind him; his Father silent before him; the first drops of many drips of blood splash to the ground. When I am tempted to believe God disinterested, Jesus models emptiness in prayer and confidence in the Father.

Today, I've come to understand granted and un-granted prayers in a way that weaves itself into my life, between my desires and God's, wrestling on the ledge of God's story.

Rich Mullins once outlined the essential characters for telling the Gospel story. God is necessary, so is Jesus. Mary needs to birth Jesus. Corrupt religious leaders to accuse him; Judas to betray; Pilate to sentence; a centurion to nail him up. Of all the people needed in the pivotal turnings of the story, few were good people. God didn't need eleven of the disciples to make the story happen. Yet Mark says "Jesus called to him those he wanted."[37] For us, it is better to be wanted by Jesus than to be needed by Jesus.

I think of petitions in that way. They are more wanted by God than needed. They align us with him. And when aligned, they may even change his actions to make us a part of them. Perhaps when aligned, the seeking and the finding go hand in hand. Jesus took the cup that would not pass from him. He knocked on the door of the will of God and it was opened to him.

He knocked on the door of the will of God and it was opened to him.

If God has mapped out human history, if he knows every tick of the clock and how to bring all to an apocalyptic climax, most details in our everyday lives are not needed to bring his story to an end. Many of the people and actions needed for his grand finale will not be changed by our prayers, no matter how fervent we are. Nor do we know the stories he has for those we love and how they are wanted in other ways, in other places. We've barely plumbed the meaning of how even suffering of the worst kind cannot separate them from his love.[38]

Along the way, we pray for things less crucial to his larger story. Many of these God grants out of his sheer pleasure of working with us. We see it happen and we note his hand (as if the whole point was to notice his hand!). James says, "You do not have because you do not ask God."[39] His works are acts of abundant grace when his children reach out to bring his goodness into the world. We do not get to see if these acts would have happened without our prayer. But we can be confident that without our prayer, we would be unable to say we, along with God, were part of it.

This allows me to trust that God is not only in control of the cosmos to the last syllable of time, but he is willing to act in my sphere of influence. He lets my actions create small changes in the world, and my prayers too. Ultimately my burden is made lighter knowing that when my prayers are un-granted, God is up to something

[38]Romans 8:28-39
[39]James 4:2

else. I may be intersecting with an
essential thread of the grand human
story, seeing his finger traced in time,
his plan marching to the cadence of his
voice. We see his plans in a glimpse,
like praying to meet our neighbor and
then immediately they are at our door
with a welcome tray of cookies; or praying for a right
response in an open forum and it, spontaneously, rides
in on a separate train of thought. Or God's hand, though
not saving my mother's life, preserving her life far longer
than the doctors expected. In these things I notice the
golden thread of God's work playing out and my little
parts in the play.

We can offer thanks for un-granted prayers, for his
invitation to glimpse the larger story. When my mother
died, I grieved, but took comfort knowing I could release
her—like an airport goodbye—for a later reunion. After
all, would I want him to answer prayers that interfered
with his plans? Would I want to prevent my mother the
joy of relief from pain, of sitting at the feet of the Lion of
Judah, of welcoming the saints as they arrive, and of her
splendid resurrection on the last day? How could I not
step back from my desires and celebrate the fulfilling of
hers?

Your Kingdom come, your will be done![40]

The last time my dying mother looked at me, when she
mustered her strength to turn her head to my voice, was
when I opened the Scriptures and read this line, "And I
saw a new Heaven and a new earth!"[41] How could any of
my most triumphant prayers keep her from that?

[40]*Matthew 6:10*
[41]*Revelation 21:1*

We can take assurance that even the Son of God had un-granted prayers. "Take this cup from me." For this un-granted prayer granted a billion prayers of others for ultimate deliverance from evil and death. The cross carried the best purposes for our planet, purposes we needed before any prayer was ever breathed.

Even the Son of God had un-granted prayers.

God Wants the Broken (video)
By Dale and Jonalyn Fincher

"**God Wants the Broken**" *by Jonalyn Fincher*

soulation.org/broken

One of the places I found myself the most broken was after my wedding got cancelled, my engagement broken off. This valley became the place God met me. Since our King bore our griefs, he is the best place for us to bring our pain in this life.[42] Listen to find out how God treasures broken people.

---

[42]*Isaiah 53:4*

FRIDAY

Death is an evil.
That's what the gods think.
Or they would die.

Sappho
Greek poet

They gave him a cross,
not guessing that he would make it a throne.

James S. Stewart
Scottish preacher

Jesus suffers at the hands of leaders and soldiers,
who lead him to Golgotha where he is
put to death on a cross.

Matthew 27

Please note that four readings saturate this day to help you soak in the
depths Jesus faced. We suggest intentional space between readings. We
recommend one upon rising, one over lunch, one before dinner,
and one at bedtime.

Healing the Soul
By Dale Fincher

While my mother was battling cancer, I took a lingering journey into the problem of suffering. As I fell into step with my mother as best I could, many thoughts flooded me over the plague of sin upon humankind, the exemption of no one, and the inevitability of death.

I turned repeatedly to the Scriptures for safe places of comfort and hope. One place in the life of Jesus stayed with me, found in Mark's opening chapters. As any writer knows, the first line, paragraph, and chapter are critical to capturing an audience's attention. And here in the first chapter, Mark begins to paint a portrait of the Messiah that is startling and shrewd.[43]

Jesus heals Peter's mother-in-law in Capernaum. Shortly afterward, many in the town bring the sick and demon-possessed to be healed by Jesus. Jesus toils "after sunset," healing the bodies of diseased victims. He heals all night for, "while it was still dark," Jesus goes to a quiet place to be with his Father. Meanwhile down in the town, more people come to be cured. The disciples find Jesus alone and say, "Everyone is looking for you!"

The world has found universal health care!

The world has found universal health care! But Jesus gives a halting reply, "Let us go somewhere else—to the nearby villages—so I can preach there also. That is why I have come."

I can imagine the faces of these new followers of Jesus.

[43]*Mark 1:29-38*

Confusion registering in their eyes. Perhaps their minds suddenly seize on that word "preach." *How is THAT going to cure anyone?* they think.

But Jesus understood something that the disciples, and even we, forgot. All healed people will become sick again. The blind will become blind again, if not in life, at least in death. And death, ultimately, will come.

Death comes if Jesus does not preach. But Jesus knew that there was something that needed healing far more than the body. Healing was needed for the soul—the desperate soul, full of brokenness, destitute with mediocre relationships, afraid of being exposed, resentful of others, dishonest with its own condition, and hiding from God in the prison of its own ego. The body would be restored, through resurrection, once the soul was bathed, born, and made alive to God.

If the souls of men and women did not find the good news Jesus was bringing into the world, then even if all the broken bodies in the world were healed, it would be of no account.

No act of defense on his part would cure the soul of his accusers.

On Friday morning, Jesus waited for his death, interrogated by Pontius Pilate. He was silent. No act of defense on his part would cure the soul of his accusers. While his enemies schemed tortures and swayed public opinion against Jesus, our Messiah could have used his heavenly powers to call down the angel of death to lay flat this mocking court. During the wait, I'm sure he thought the same words he used at the start of Mark, "This is why I have come."

Back at the scene of preaching to the people who insisted on being healed, Jesus stood his ground with the disciples and insisted that, instead of physical healing, there must be a spiritual healing of the souls of men and women across the countryside of Israel. "THAT is why I have come," he said. And he went out proclaiming the news that, finally, the way to friendship with Jehovah had been opened and a more lasting healing was on the way. He preached and preached all the way to the cross where he would then unbalance all the powers that bring sickness and death.

Refocus Through Suffering
By Dale Fincher

Under a sunny spring sky, my sister-in-law treated us to a day at Disneyland. My two-year-old son loved riding the teacups, but spelunking the caves on Tom Sawyer's Island stole him away. I tracked him up and down and around dark corners where he found ladders, forts, and pirate treasure.

Outside, as we waited to board Tom Sawyer's raft, we watched a water bird swimming in the lagoon. The bird split the water with his heron-like beak and dove. When it emerged, a fish wiggled on its beak, speared through the middle. Not a minnow, but a fish three times the size of the bird's head. All of us waiting at the dock, maybe 30 guests, turned to the bird, an attraction we didn't pay to see. We watched the fish struggle on the harpoon poking through its center, slapping its fins, while the soundtrack of utopian Disney played in the background.

Then the bird twirled the fish on its beak and opened wide. It gulped the fish large throated. The crowd gasped.

The polished world of Disney—the cajun-dressed banjo band, the artificial rocks and cement trees, and the house that isn't haunted—could not keep real life from breaking into this moment. A rogue bird reminded us that the gritty world cannot be ignored.

Our modern world fills us with illusion that more technology, faster movies, fashion, medicine, and government oversight will create utopia. Yet even Disneyland cannot hide fish speared by

Our modern world fills us with illusion.

a bird, guests burdened with cancer, and children who came to the amusement park with their grandparents because their parents are "having problems."

No matter what we fabricate to distract us into forgetting our pain and keep our feet from feeling the earth, real things keep breaking our spells. Beauty and evil, happiness and suffering, pleasure and disappointment all remain. While Jesus was tried by the Sanhedrin and sent from one ruler to another, the world kept moving. Jewish families prepared for the Sabbath. Herod, no doubt, enjoyed a delicious breakfast. Pilate's wife may have been enjoying a massage to ward off her horrible night's rest. While Jesus was beaten, fish were caught and sold in Galilee. False promises of a new *shalom* kept chugging forward under the Roman occupation. And Jesus was mocked to fulfill God's promise of a redeemed future.

Real things keep breaking our spells.

When we first moved to Steamboat Springs, Colorado from Los Angeles, I thought I had found an unspoiled place, a small town with less concrete, fewer power lines, and no suburbs. Few places are as idyllic to me as the rolling Yampa Valley bordered by mountains, which looks like a home for hobbits who want to try alpine skiing. I was walking through town the first week of our move and heard a car drive by playing loud music. Big city pop music. Digitized, unnatural music. My first thought, "He should turn off his music and listen to nature with his windows down!" My idealism for my new hometown felt slightly shaken.

Then I heard reports of suicides and rapes and even news of a former teacher from the local Christian school being charged with molesting a student in town.

The real world crashes in, no matter our hopes for the beauty around us. We can eat our Disney cotton candy but we can't be fooled to think this is the happiest place on earth. We can move to small town America and know evil will find us here, including our own. In the seemingly insignificant life of Mary, a heroine was born. She faced the rumors of her firstborn's legitimacy, and she faced the real world of her son beaten beyond her recognition. She traveled to witness his painful walk with his cross to Golgotha, bent over by the glory of Rome.

For thousands of years, God saw the excruciating predicament and the powerlessness of humanity. He knows the task calls for the Everlasting Hero.

> Dost ask who that may be?
> Christ Jesus, it is He;
> Lord Sabaoth[44] His name,
> From age to age the same,
> And He must win the battle.

He knows the task calls for the Everlasting Hero.

This is the story of the cross, where the vertical and horizontal beams serve as a signpost of the meeting of heaven and earth, the ideal reaching the real. Where God looked upon the mess of this world and instead of snatching us away humming "It's a Small World After All," he stepped into it and called for a broom. Not to demolish, but to remodel. He took us, pockmarked, not to airbrush us smooth, but to scour us of dirt. Not to make us something else, but to make us ourselves.

This is our hope. I'm reminded of the film *The Passion*, where Jesus stumbles and his mother runs to him. "Behold," he says with the bearing of a king, "I am making all things new."

[44]"Lord Sabaoth" means "Lord of armies"

The Day the King Died
By Dale Fincher

On that Friday, before Sabbath, Pilate nailed a sign above Jesus' head. It read, "Jesus of Nazareth, The King of the Jews."[45] Jesus was mocked for declaring himself King, though other kings killed over his power, even as a baby.[46] But Jesus, as King of the Jews, was King of Heaven and Earth. King Jesus was the rightful heir to the throne of David. He came as one of the chosen people, to fulfill the Jewish work to repair the world. He, like his people, was a light to the nations and the bearer of good news that the God of Israel had come near.

More than any other title, the Gospel writers remind us that Jesus is Messiah, the anointed King of the Jews. "Who do you say that I am?" Jesus asks his disciples.

"You are the Messiah [King of the Jews], Son of the living God," replies Peter.[47]

On the heels of that statement, Jesus tells his students about the day the King would die.[48]

Jesus tells his students about the day the King would die.

Now the moment had come on that dark Friday. Just like all of us, the King died too. But like a warrior at battle, this King died for others.

We step closer and closer to the grave.

From the moment we are born, we step closer and closer to the grave. It seems unnatural but it is inescapable.

[45]*John 19:19*   [47]*Matthew 16:15-16*
[46]*Matthew 2:1-18*   [48]*Matthew 16:21-28*

The most prevailing argument against Christianity is the problem of evil. Many atheists, from the ancient Epicurus to the modern Richard Dawkins, say the problem of evil led to their disbelief in God. If God were lovingly powerful, he would stop evil. But since evil does exist, then God must not possess those divine qualities.

When Jesus hung on the cross, he appeared to shout an atheistic argument. He cried out, "My God, my God, why have you forsaken me?"[49] Many theologians have assumed this is the moment when God was powerless, when the Father could not look upon his own Son.

However, a look at the source of these words shows us that Jesus was quoting a king in his family tree whose throne he would one day claim. "My God, my God, why have you forsaken me?" are the opening lines of David's Psalm 22. At this point in the crucifixion Jesus is sapped of strength and facing asphyxiation. He can only draw breath by pushing on the nails in his feet to expand his flattened lungs to gulp air. Jesus' words were brief because they had to be. He was incapable of quoting the psalm in its entirety. But like Rabbis of his time, quoting the opening phrases of a passage was an abbreviation of the whole passage. Jesus knew that great suffering did not mean great abandonment. Read Psalm 22 to get an idea of the answer to the problem of evil, a God who

> has not despised or scorned
>> the suffering of the afflicted one;
> he has not hidden his face from him
>> but has listened to his cry for help.[50]

[49]*Matthew 27:46*
[50]*Psalm 22:24*

God does not stop all pain, suffering, and even death, nor does he promise to. He never promised that all struggles would cease here, that all heartache would stop today. He has already come but the fullness of his promises are not fully here.

The fullness of his promises are not fully here.

God obligated himself to something bigger, to dig out the largest root of the problem. Jesus came to conquer our final and ultimate foe—death—and make our souls fit for God. And Jesus conquered with the wisdom and nimble plot twist of a master Ruler, using the instrument of a Roman cross.

My wife says that when Christ suffered on the cross, he dignified all of our suffering. When Christ died, he dignified our deaths too. Not because he takes suffering away, but because he joins us in it. Paul says that we get to share in the fellowship of his suffering.[51] Peter says that Christ suffered for sins that he might bring us to God.[52]

That's why Paul often refers to death for the saints as a mere "sleep." Death's arrow was blunted, the coffin has lost.[53]

Death is not really the grand finale. It is a consequence of being a rebellious race. Through Adam, the rebellion affected not just our souls but our bodies. The consequence of death is like the consequence of burning your finger on a flame. You learn quickly how tragic the incident, but you must also face the blister.

Death is a severe mercy to bring us into a quality of life that is everlasting. For those who trust Jesus Christ as the cure of our infirmity, death is a pivotal part of the healing

[51]Philippians 3:10
[52]1 Peter 3:18
[53]1 Corinthians 15:55

process. Death is like a caterpillar's cocoon. It transforms us. It sheds us of the old so that, through the coming resurrection, we have a new life. Death is a passing through the gate of the wilderness into the courtyard of the palace garden. We need new bodies, just like the entire earth needs to be remade,[54] so we can return to walking with God in the cool of the garden.[55]

Death is like a caterpillar's cocoon.

The famed pastor, Joseph Bayly, reflecting on his own ailing child in the hospital wired with tubes and masks, offers us this biblical hope:

> If You should take him home
> to Your home
> help me then remember
> how Your Son suffered
> and You stood by
> watching
> agonizing watching
> waiting
> to bring all suffering to an end
> forever
> on a day
> yet to be.[56]

He forgave his killers and spilled his blood to wash their sin.

The King is the Lord of all things, even over death. Bearing a thorny crown, he forgave his killers and spilled his blood to wash their sin. With three simple words, he plunged straightaway into the dominion of death and darkness to break every last chain: It is finished.[57]

[54]*Revelation 21:1*
[55]*Genesis 3:8*
[56]*From Joseph Bayly,* The Last Thing We Talk About, *Revised Edition*
[57]*John 19:30*

Prepping our Souls
By Dale Fincher

From the Garden of Gethsemane, through Jesus' final breath at execution, shock ran through everyone that followed Jesus. The late afternoon arrived and Sabbath was coming. They broke the legs of the thieves. But they only pierced Jesus because he was already dead.[58] A rich man, Joseph, a dissenting voice on the Council who spoke up against the killing of Jesus, asked Pilate for the body of the King and laid Jesus nearby in his own tomb.[59] Nicodemus also brought spices and helped in wrapping the body according to Jewish burial customs.[60]

The last smells of death faded. The disciples scattered in grief. The women closest to Jesus saw the tomb and went home to prepare spices for the body. But as the sun set they knew they would have to wait for Sabbath to pass. Sabbath was the deep sigh of time, where everything, even death-making and death-preparing, stopped. Only silence for a long, hollow day of grief. Silence that felt, I'm sure, as cold as death itself.

Death was familiar to the ancients. It lingered around them in the brutalities of war and in sicknesses at home. They had no hospitals or convalescent homes for their sick or old to be hidden. Watching a body move from warmth to coldness all happened at home. When the final breath was taken, many witnessed the passing.

> Death is like a caterpillar's cocoon.

[58]*John 19:31-37*
[59]*Luke 23:50-53*
[60]*John 19: 39-40*

63

These first century people were also honest about death's approach. Throughout the Bible, death is spoken of as a common thing. Death was often less important than allegiance. For what will you die? With whom will you align yourself in life and in death? Though death was undesirable, it was part of a bigger picture.

Because of this, many knew that one of the goals in this life was to prepare for the next. Not to leave a dazzling obituary behind, but to be holy. To walk blameless. To deepen your life in the teachings of the Law and the Prophets and to be the fruitful tree King David talked about in Psalm 1. There was something more at stake and death was another way to notice what mattered.

Today we drown out the fear of death with a mocking denial of it. Joseph Bayly, who lost all his sons in his lifetime, says, "The sort of taboo Victorians placed on public discussion of sex has been transferred to death in our culture."[61] Not only do we sideline its ugliness to hospitals, but we also simulate an artificial fear of it in our horror movies. After the movie is over, we walk back into our ordinary lives, something death never permits. We see death so often on the silver screen and the plasma TV, that it has become trivial. I wonder, though, how many of us sit regularly, as those who followed Jesus, considering how frail life is and that our purposes here are bigger than merely getting by or entertaining ourselves to escape life's difficulties.

Let us imagine how sleepless the disciples were that night in the city hushed with Sabbath. Could they sleep? They had lost their friend and teacher, their poet and healer, their purpose and future. Let us set our purposes, like the women, toward preparation in our souls. Let us sit in the

[61]From Joseph Bayly, The Last Thing We Talk About, *Revised Edition*

quiet that rumbles with hope. It's over. Jesus is dead. His blood spilled on the altar of the world to cover our sins. But nobody knew what it meant.

In a sealed tomb, with his body still, Jesus rested from his labor.

In a sealed tomb, with his body still, Jesus rested from his labor.

While the city practiced Sabbath, the enemies of Jesus posted a guard of soldiers at the tomb to prevent thieves from stealing the body.[62] While they worried about their political stories and their plans, God drew his people into unhurried silence of communion with himself. He held the keys to the meaning of all that happened. We must sit in the silence too. Sabbath has come.

[62]*Matthew 27:62-65*

SATURDAY

We sit across the dining table,
You ask me what I'm doing,
"I'm giving this moment some dignity."

Amy Kaneko
American poet

Jesus' body lays in the tomb while his disciples
observe the Sabbath,

a day of rest.

Something is coming, but first,
a day of silence.

A poem.

A morning meditation on practical rest.

An afternoon reflection on life-giving silence.

Luke 23:55-56
Exodus 20:8-11

Let It Open
By Amy Kaneko

Notice the subtleties,
the way crimson tides
slosh smooth in a crystal planet.

This world is a gift; you must let it open.

Swirl and swirl and swirl,
don't be pretentious.
Wine's Law of Gravity states
you must let your head
weigh down till nostrils plunge
into oaken atmospheres;
Inhale heavy.

Come up for air before you drown
in cabernet tidal waves.

Breathe it in heavier yet.
Drink it down,
slow,
let it flood a deluge
on your tongue.

Lather, rinse, repeat.

Grab a pen, spill it out, stain that page wine-red.

We sit across the dining table,
you ask me what I'm doing,
"I'm giving this moment some dignity."[63]

[63]Used by permission. Find Amy Kaneko's biography
and website on page 96. 67

Invitation to Rest
By Jonalyn Fincher

Jerusalem was quiet on the day after Jesus' death. No one gathered spices for the tomb. Jews rested to honor the Sabbath. Even after the greatest drama in world history, the death of the Son of God, there is silence, long and restful, space for the mess of tears unchecked. Time to consider before another big work on Sunday morning would begin.

Sometimes I wonder if Jesus didn't rise from the dead on the Sabbath because even he rested from all his work, like a deep breath before life overshadowed all darkness forever.

The first thing God called holy wasn't a person or an animal, it wasn't a star or a plant; it was a day, a wedge of time.[64] On the seventh day of creation, God comes to a surprising halt.[65] If I were having as much fun as God with all that creativity, I'm not sure I'd want to stop.

Free from productivity, the God of Israel opened up a palace of time for himself, and walked right in, put his feet up, and took his ease.[66]

> The God of Israel opened up a palace of time for himself.

In our busy Western world, rest is something we do if we have the leisure, and even those of us who are not worried about food and shelter still find ourselves busy, always rushing. We imagine that the

[64]*Genesis 2:3*
[65]*Genesis 1:31-2:3*
[66]*This idea of a palace in time comes from Abraham Heschel's* The Sabbath.

wealthy rest, the lazy rest, but those of us worth admiring have real work, real lives, families, young children, sick relatives, churches, hobbies, and vacation time we're storing up. We do not rest. We've found a way to cope with caffeine, to relax on the drive, to pray while we work out, to pack it all in. As one erroneous Christian slogan says, "When I'm dead, I'll rest."

Most of us believe rest is for the weary and faint, the overwhelmed, the sick or depressed, and those lacking the passion to do God's work. We rest because we're forced into it, not because we're invited.

It's pretty hard to even imagine what a day of rest at home without a beach and a tropical drink would look like. How do you rest in the clutter and unfinished business of home? Isn't true rest like good sex? Something you have to go on vacation to find?

The Sabbath between the King's death and the King's rise is a once-in-a-year chance to notice how to rest.

Rest is as spiritually significant to God as prayer. But I know that, in our success-driven world, it is easier and even more rewarding to pray. You can point to that time as productive, focused, self-disciplined. It's even easier to fast (especially with the added perk of losing a few pounds) or to give to the poor. Rest does not come with spiritual adrenaline included or any bragging rights.

> Rest is as spiritually significant to God as prayer.

Nevertheless, we find resting, along with other timeless commands, lodged in the Ten Commandments, between honoring God's name and our parents. God was such a big supporter of rest he rained extra manna (complete with preservatives) the day before the Sabbath so the Israelites could have breakfast, lunch, and dinner without having to work to gather their food. [67]

Any week that I accept God's invitation to enter the Sabbath, I'm walking into a palace of time. And at the end of those 24 hours, I feel luxuriously back to who I am. I'm so full and calm. I've drunk of the river of his delights because I've found the path to sit by this stream, again.[68]

And what do I have to show for the time? I've watched the chickadees scatter seed on the snow and my son scatter his toys. I've watched the dishes and the laundry pile up. And I know the world is still turning, my world is still intact, God is still the light of my life.[69]

God is still the light of my life.

For this Sabbath, take a moment to find what rest and work look like in your life. You might begin with one intuitive question, "What feels like work to me?"

Here's a list of what work looks like in my world:

1. writing
2. responding to emails
3. outlining a public address
4. laundry
5. dusting
6. cleaning toilets or dishes
7. any cleaning, actually
8. going online
9. shopping
10. discussing business

[67]*Exodus 16:22-26*
[68]*Psalm 36:8*
[69]*Psalm 36:9*

Now, the fun question, "What would I do if I knew all my work was done?"

What would I do if I knew all my work was done?

Of course, this requires a stretch of the imagination, but go with me. Imagine that all the items on the first list were completed. An empty inbox, a paper turned in, a sparkling toilet, a clear counter, stocked shelves.

Now what?

A nap!

Okay, take it.

Then, you wake up. You ask yourself again, "What would I do if I knew all my work was done?" My answers are windows into my day of rest.

1. watch an hour of 30 Rock
2. spontaneously play with my son
3. sit on the porch
4. a long, hot bath
5. poetry over lunch
6. slowly, carefully make macaroni and cheese
7. watercolor
8. snowshoe on my own
9. pray
10. read Scripture slowly, maybe just two verses

Each Sabbath is a gathering, not a scattering, of minutes. Rest requires that I overlook the things that working people everywhere feel obliged to fix: dusty baseboards, crumbs on the

I overlook the things that working people everywhere feel obliged to fix.

floor, piles of snow at my doorstep, food-covered dishes, overflowing inboxes, buzzing phones. And yes, even the meals might be less healthy and organized, as everyone scrounges for themselves. Sure, the house will be dirtier, and the lists of things to do will be longer tomorrow. You might even feel curious whether you're still valuable at the end of the day.

Good and well. Bring that to God. Let rest be something you do, not to optimize your ability to work, not to obey an ancient command, but as a way to learn who God made you to be without your work bolstering your value and identity.

Leave the sanctity of Sabbath, that palace of rest, ready to celebrate the King who will soon rise with healing in his wings.

Life-Giving Silence

By Dale Fincher

"Muzak" is the noise we hear on the telephone after an operator puts us on hold. It is sometimes called "elevator music." Muzak is everywhere, even our own homes. Journalist Mike Zwerin put it this way, "Walk into just about any public urban space—supermarkets, restaurants, sports stadiums, airports—and you will hear the aggressive sonic wallpaper known as background music—the increasingly inescapable soundtrack of our lives."[70] He concludes that our Western culture has been "murdering silence with bad music."

This is not the only way we have murdered silence. Malcolm Muggeridge coined the phrase "Newzak" to reference all the meaningless news that airs on video screens everywhere we go. It is not really news intended to be watched with our minds engaged. It is mostly entertainment that parades itself with flashy colors and modes of immediacy. In reality, ignoring Newzak is like avoiding used bubblegum on a Manhattan sidewalk. We hardly notice anymore. Yet the noise still remains, even if we ignore it.

The virus of noise in our society has been a daily habit. Apple earned the status of most valuable company in the world on the backbone of iTunes and the iPods and iPhones linked to it.

> We want a soundtrack for our lives.

How many of us actually leave the car stereo off during our daily commute? For many of us, to drive in silence is an unknown torture that causes our inner life to squirm.

[70]*Mike Zwerin,* "Murdering Silence with Bad Music," *International Herald Tribune, Dec 29, 2004*

We want a soundtrack for our lives.

I remember the time when thieves stole the stereo from my car. I drove for six weeks without any sound. Because I was unable to listen to music or news, the silence broke the habit of noise in my life. I found an oasis. The quiet in my car became a sudden vacation, a Sabbath from music.

What does noise mean for a soul that is supposed to walk in peace with God, to enter the fellowship of his sufferings, and listen to the subtleties of the Holy Spirit's still voice? How does silence change our soul? I think the noise, no matter how "spiritual" it sounds, can sometimes hinder us from attending to the most important thing. Murdering silence may be strangling our souls.

> Murdering silence may be strangling our souls.

The disciples huddled together in silence on the Sabbath to think and grieve. They replayed the events, I'm sure, the stories, parables, and the spiritual insights. They must have wondered if it mattered anymore. Were they already talking of the "next thing"? The women were eyeing the spices they prepared, waiting for sunrise to carry them to the cemetery. How would the Sons of Thunder replace their Messiah with fishing again? How would Matthew go back to accounting? Peter would try to fish again, reliving, perhaps with every throw of his net, the words of the dead teacher, "I will make you fishers or men."

> They would consider all these things and weep.

In the silence of the Sabbath, they would consider all these things and weep.

I believe one reason why many of us are addicted to perpetual noise is that we do not want to hear the cry of our own souls. The fear, resentment, regret, dishonesty, or selfishness may be so loud on the inside, we try to drown it out with noise from the outside. How reluctant we are to invite Jesus into that suffering, for him to sit with us and mend us and comfort us.

Meanwhile, the Messiah continues to call us. We hear him say from the cross: "It is finished."[71] We hear him say along the road, "Come to me, all you who are weary and burdened, and I will give you rest. Take my yoke upon you and learn from me, for I am gentle and humble in heart, and you will find rest for your souls."[72]

How different our lives may be if we silenced our souls with Christ's rest rather than perpetual noise. The psalmist admonishes us, "When you are on your beds, search your hearts and be silent."[73] Try to silence the music for this Sabbath, between the cross and the empty tomb. May God meet us today as we choose to open our souls and our ears to that voice that lies on the other side of silence.

Try to silence the music for this Sabbath

[71]John 19:30
[72]Matthew 11:28-29
[73]Psalm 4:4

SUNDAY

"The last chapter of the human story is not death but life. Jesus' resurrection guarantees it."

Gerald Sittser
American author, spiritual director

Mary Magdalene finds an empty tomb,
but her confusion and grief soon turns to joy
when Jesus appears and proves the dead king is alive.

Matthew 18
John 20
Matthew 28

The First Witness[74]
By Dale and Jonalyn Fincher

In John 20, you can read about the first person to walk upon Jesus alive and healed. Her experience bears entering into as we imagine what the resurrection must have meant to someone like Mary Magdalene.

If Mary of Magdala could have spoken about what Jesus did for her, she might talk about a Rabbi, a Teacher who healed her. We've imagined the stories Mary would have told herself as she walked to the tomb, stories she learned by listening to Mary of Bethany and following Jesus along with his other disciples. Imagine her world as we watch the sun rise on resurrection Sunday.

I have not learned the Law. My father would quote the Jewish teaching, "Sooner let the words of the Law be burnt than delivered to women."

I remember when I was very little how my brother would return from school and impress me by quoting his lessons. One sticks in my mind: "Happy is he whose children are males, and woe to him whose children are females." Then he'd point at me, "You bring our Abba unhappiness."

As my brother grew, he learned the more weighty matters of the law. From him I learned that women are not permitted to speak up or testify in court because of our

[74]To hear a dramatized retelling of Mary Magdalene's story, listen to soulation.org/broken.

frailty and inability to resist bribes. It is written that our testimony is as worthless as a criminal's.

But the rabbis do not all agree about women. It is even said that one rabbi, the Teacher, Jesus of Nazareth, permitted women to learn from him.

Mary of Bethany told me her story. She once entered the room where the Teacher was speaking, leaving her duties of preparing the food, walking past the disapproving stares and clicking tongues, through the dusty feet of Jesus' disciples, and sat down in an empty place, at his feet, where every man in the room could see her.

She refused to move, listening to the Rabbi's teaching. And Jesus did not tell her to leave. Her older sister, Martha, came with fire in her eyes and raised her voice creating enough noise to send any little sister running back to her post. When Mary stood up to obey, the Teacher stopped her. He said Mary did not have to return to the kitchen. Then he added, "Mary has chosen the good part, the best thing to do. And no one will take that away from her."

I would like to be like Mary of Bethany.

I would like to be like Mary of Bethany. But the only similarity between us is our name. She was never harassed by the demons as I was.

Since I was a young girl many beautiful angelic beings would appear and tell me to do evil things. I would obey them, because they threatened me that my mother would die if I did not heed their words.

It was Jesus who released me from them.

Since that day, I left my family and have followed Jesus from afar, waiting in the shadows, making food for his disciples, hoping for a chance to learn more.

It was Jesus who released me.

If my family had heard of my hopes to learn at the Teacher's feet, they would have claimed that the demons had returned. They would have taken me away. So I held myself back, and for two years I continued to rehearse Mary's story. "Choose the good part," she would say, "choose Jesus and he will not be taken away from you."

But he was taken.

But he was taken. Jesus was taken by our own leaders, the Jewish teachers and scribes, and taken to the Sanhedrin. Then he was taken from them to Pilate, then to Herod, then to Pilate, and then to Golgotha. Then his dignity was taken, his strength, his blood, his energy, and when he only had his life, it was taken too. He was killed there in front of every man and woman and child traveling that road.

I saw him die.

Two days later, after Sabbath, I walked to the tomb so early I could barely see. The light was just beginning to spread its rosy color on the graves.

When I reached his tomb, the stone was rolled aside from the opening and the dark cavity was exposed. Anyone could have further tortured his body. I ran to it, but his body wasn't there. Who would have unwrapped his mangled body? Where had they put him?

I ran from the place to get help. Peter and John were the only two I could find. They barely looked at me, rushing past to run to the tomb. Though I tried to keep up, they were too fast. By the time I reached the tomb, they had fled. And I was left alone again, standing at his tomb, bewildered, exhausted, crying.

I stooped inside the tomb and then, I saw them. They were waiting for me, two large, shining beings, calmly sitting inside his tomb. One asked me why I was crying. I felt my heart jump with fear. What did they want from me? The demons…had they returned?

I slowly backed out of the tomb telling them, "They took my Teacher away and I don't know where they put him." Then a voice hemmed me in from behind with the same question: "Why are you crying?"

Unwilling to take my eyes off the ones in the tombs, I pleaded with the man behind me, "Sir, if you have taken him away from here, show me where he is. I will get him and bring him back."

But before I could turn around, the man said the only thing that, surrounded by tombs and strangers, could have touched my frantic feelings.

"Mary."

I froze. Ten thoughts raced through my head: How did he know my name? It must be one of the disciples. Peter or John? But the voice was like…the Teacher when he called me out from the demons, so familiar and so confident.

"Mary."

I turned…and cried out, "Teacher!" I sunk down to the ground, undone with amazement, joy, safety, relief. He was here; the demons wouldn't claim me. He was here; he was real. He was real and alive. I was kneeling at the feet of the Rabbi Jesus. And he was alive. He was breathing and standing and talking to me. I reached out to touch his feet.

He was real and alive.

Was he really alive? Was I dreaming this? Were these the demons again?

No ghost is so substantial.

His feet were real. I could feel them. I could see the scarred holes where the nails had pierced his flesh. No ghost is so substantial.

I wanted to stay, to sit at his feet, to listen to him. But Jesus wouldn't let me. He gave me my first instructions that morning.

"Mary, let go of my feet. Go, tell them, tell my brothers, 'I am returning to my Father and your Father, to my God and your God.'"

I wouldn't have left him unless he told me to. As I raced from the tomb in search of his disciples I wondered at him trusting me. He thought I could deliver his message. He trusted the woman of Magdala, the woman who had hosted demons in her body, the woman the disciples ignored. The Teacher had come to me and he had sent me to them.

I ran all the way to the disciples' home. The first words on my lips must have sounded like the ranting of a wild woman, but I didn't care. Jesus had told me to tell them. I threw open the door.

"I have seen him; I have seen the Teacher!" And they stopped and listened to me, Mary Magdalene, a follower of Christ.

I have seen him; I have seen the Teacher!

We believe the tomb is empty, that Jesus broke the power of death and walked out of the cemetery. How do we know this? We may say, "It's in the Bible," but many people who want to believe are not satisfied with this answer. Many need to know that what the Bible says is true and not invented.

How would someone know if the New Testament writers were telling the truth? There are many signposts that indicate the truth of their message that even secular scholars apply to secular ancient manuscripts, from Plato to Thucydides. Let's look at one of them: the Embarrassment Test.[75]

The Embarrassment Test says that if someone were inventing a story, they would not include details that hurt the story in an embarrassing way. For example, if we wrote an autobiography on modeling safe driving, we would leave out details of speeding tickets, parking

[75]*This easy-to-read book,* The Case for the Resurrection of Jesus *by Gary Habermas and Michael Licona, has much more on the historicity of Jesus' resurrection. We recommend it.*

violations, and failures to use a turn signal. If we did include those stories, most readers would likely conclude that 1) we are not models of safe driving, and 2) those stories of traffic violations were probably the most reliable parts of the story. Why? Because it hurts our case.

Scholars see such stories in ancient writings and conclude the same thing.

Let's give a biblical example of the Embarrassment Test. Who was the leading spokesman after the Holy Spirit came upon the disciples in Acts 2? Peter. Do we know anything embarrassing about Peter?

He failed to walk on water for very long. He cut off a servant's ear. He insisted a tent be set up for Elijah and Moses on the Mount of Transfiguration. He denied Jesus three times.

And when Jesus told his disciples he would be flogged and killed in Jerusalem, Peter told Jesus he was wrong. Then Jesus replied to Peter, "Get behind me, Satan."

If you're going to invent a story to dupe the whole world with a new religion, you avoid calling your leading spokesman "Satan."

The stories of Peter are not invented stories. These are embarrassing details which validate Peter's story and his later remarkable change (and Peter's embarrassing moments continue in the New Testament).

How about women in the ancient world? The public saw them as second-class citizens. They couldn't hold public office. They weren't allowed to testify in a court of law, for their testimonies were gullible and no better than that of a common criminal. Today we know not to see women are equal to mean, but Jesus' contemporaries would not have agreed with us.

As we look at the resurrection of Jesus, who do we find at the empty tomb of Jesus first? If this story were fabricated, we'd see a scholar, a member of the Sanhedrin, or maybe a professor from the University of Jerusalem. Those examples would give a "reliable" witness to all that happened. Instead, the biblical writers—all of them—report women at the tomb first.

That's embarrassing. The only reason to write this kind of story is because that is the way it actually happened. Truth is, one Sunday morning a small group of women, carrying spices, went to the tomb where Jesus was laid and found it empty. Let's go running like Mary Magdalene and shout that he's alive!

As we bask in the soul-refreshing hope that Jesus wrestled with death and won, we take confidence that Jesus is not just a religious pipe-dream that we wish were true. Jesus is alive and the evidence supports it.

Jesus wrestled with death and won.

Long Live the King
By Dale Fincher

A tomb sealed quietly in Bethany near Jerusalem, the victory of death over the body of a man. Two sisters wept, Mary and Martha, surrounded by professional mourners.[76]

On the outskirts of town, Jesus finally arrived with his band of men. The sisters blamed Jesus for not coming sooner. They knew he had the power to heal. Why didn't he come and heal? He had healed many strangers. Why didn't he come heal a friend?

Jesus, composed and determined, said, "I am the resurrection and the life. The one who believes in me will live, even though they die; and whoever lives by believing in me will never die. Do you believe this?" Martha's reply reveals that she did not understand his power or purpose, but she did know he was trustworthy: "I believe that you are the Messiah, the Son of God, who is to come into the world."

Jesus weeps with them.

After the command was given to roll away the stone, Jesus prayed aloud to his Father for all to hear and then uttered the words, "Lazarus, come out!" And he came out.

Jesus weeps with them.

Suddenly the incredible power of death which paralyzed the world was broken. Death, though it had spoken volumes and silenced the lives of all humanity, did not have the last word.

Another Word was spoken.

As this Word was spoken to penetrate the power of death, many began to plot to erase that Word. This was the last miracle Jesus did. But he saved the most important miracle for three days after the cross.

He saved the most important miracle for three days after the cross.

Jesus' miracle for Lazarus had an expiration date. Lazarus would die again on another day. The Scripture is silent on the second physical death of Lazarus. But we can be assured that Lazarus, though the focal point of so much awe and scrutiny, was again laid in that tomb. The physical miracles of Jesus were always temporary ones. And the loss of a brother would come again one day to the hearts of the women.

Death's word can only be overshadowed by the permanent solution of the final Word! Lazarus' resurrection was not enough. The ultimate fulcrum of suffering and healing resides in King Jesus who bursts forth in his resurrection. God has visited our planet and not left us in sin and error. The King is on the move. His warm breath makes life flow out of cold stone. His life is a promise, the first fruits of his eternal kind of life.[77]

The King is on the move.

Long live the King!

[77] 1 Corinthians 15:20

But what does this mean for us? How does the King's new life mean life for us today?

The suffering of losing those we love lingers for a long time, even when we have everlasting hope. Gerald L. Sittser, who lost three generations of his family in one automobile accident, writes in his thoughtful book, *A Grace Disguised*,

> Suffering engenders a certain degree of ambivalence in those of us who believe in the resurrection. We feel the pain of our present circumstance, which reminds us of what we have lost; yet we hope for future release and victory. We doubt, yet try to believe; we suffer, yet long for real healing; we inch hesitantly toward death, yet see death as the door to resurrection…Living with this ambivalence is both difficult and vital. It stretches our souls, challenging us to acknowledge our morality and yet to continue to hope for final victory—the victory Jesus won for us in his death and resurrection, a victory that awaits us only on the other side of the grave.

When my mother was dying of cancer, I asked her what new treatments were available. After 11 major chemotherapies I expected she'd have strength for more. "Where's the hope?" I asked her over breakfast. She sipped on her coffee in silence. I waited for her to share new experimental drugs or the prospect of better specialists. Without pomp, she began to speak from deep wells in her soul with a realism and confidence of one who knows what it means to stand on the rock.

"The hope," she replied, "is in the resurrection."

Three months later, she bore that hope to the grave.

One day she will rise again.

Although all people die, not all people will really live. Little wonder that Paul speaks repeatedly of having our life in God.[78] In him we died, in him we live. In Jesus the King, we see time and eternity joined as our life in him is happening now. Look out your window, life is brimming and calling you. Though the body is dying, the soul is growing more alive in resurrection life day by day.[79] You and I will never die.

The soul is growing more alive in resurrection life day by day.

Sittser writes again, "The last chapter of the human story is not death but life. Jesus' resurrection guarantees it." For all who are willing to be part of Jesus' unquenchable hope and his never-ending story, we can join the kingdom of the King that men did not crown and cannot dethrone. We can bury our sorrows with the Man of Sorrows as we wait to vacate our own burial plots. Jesus our Messiah will utter, once and for all, "Come out!"

The living Jesus promises life beyond the grave. He plunges into the icy water of death like a diver searching for lost treasure. With resurrection Sunday, Jesus returns into the bright warm sun, splashing in his noon-day glory, and holding aloft the gold coin of our humanity. As the King of creation he holds the power to make good on his promises of creating a one-of-a-kind permanent place prepared for us.[80] He's the only one who has lived on both sides of reality, material and immaterial, and has returned to tell of it. He sits on his throne with all authority in

[78]Colossians 3:1-4
[79]2 Corinthians 4:16
[80]John 14:1-4

heaven and on earth.[81] We celebrate with nothing to fear, nothing to lose, and nothing to hide, when he says, *Because I live, you also will live.*[82]

May this anthem resonate deep in our souls day after day until we see the King face to face.

> Because I live, you also will live.

[81]*Matthew 28:18*
[82]*John 14:19*

Hope is Resurrection (audio)
By Dale and Jonalyn Fincher

"Hope is Resurrection" by Dale and Jonalyn Fincher

soulation.org/resurrection

Jesus conquers death and illuminates a new guarantee. We call this light "hope," and it shines forth on Resurrection Sunday with a brilliance that is meant for all humans to walk in and enjoy.

Dale and Jonalyn were invited to speak on the resurrection of Jesus at the city-wide Easter Sunrise Service in Laguna Beach, California. This audio recording takes you between theology, culture, and imagination, with dramatizations of Mary Magdalene and Doubting Thomas. Imagine the sun rising over this ocean town, sitting in the outdoor amphitheater, Christ playing in ten thousand places, and the people of God celebrating the life and promises of Jesus.

REFLECTION QUESTIONS

MONDAY

Morning

Have you found some beliefs in your spirituality or religion forcing you to change yourself to fit into what God wants for you? Choose one. Be specific.

What are some examples of beliefs that are so harmful they must be driven out? Here are two to get you started: "Some people are more equal than others" and "A leader is above the rules of honesty and integrity."

Evening

What type of person is hard for you to respect? What religious followers are more difficult for you to want to get to know?

Try to answer this question for yourself: "If God is love, how has he specifically shown his love to me?" Share your answers by telling the story surrounding the experience you had.

TUESDAY

Build on the example of being unworthy of winning
a marathon but still worthy as a human being. Use
examples of when you might be unworthy for a reward,
but still worthy as a human made in God's image.

How does this statement sit with you: "Jesus came for
those who are valuable. His coming did not make us
valuable"? List some specific examples of valuable things
in human beings.

Evening

Have you ever tracked the source of a historical object or
favorite song? Tell that story.

Share a bite of something to eat or a sip of something
to drink. How does this food or drink communicate
something about God?

WEDNESDAY

Morning

Can you think of a person who used his/her humility to make great things happen for someone else? Share what makes you think of this person as humble.

How are humility and confidence linked?

Evening

Where does the word Passover come from? What do you think Jesus felt as he ate the lamb and bread and drank the wine?

If you had a meal to share with your favorite people, who would be there?

THURSDAY

Morning

If weeping is part of being whole and human, why do so few cry? What kinds of things usually move you to cry?

Have you ever felt like God was laughing at you? Share a story of that time.

Evening

When do you believe God answered your prayer? What made you think he had answered you?

What prayers has God answered with a "no"? How do you know to keep praying or stop?

FRIDAY

Morning
Why does Jesus focus more on preaching than healing?

Midday
Have you ever been in an ideal setting when the real world came crashing in? How was the day Jesus carried his cross both ideal and real?

Dinner
Read Psalm 22. By referencing this psalm, how is Jesus showing both pain and hope in his words from the cross?

Night
Have you ever faced death? What about the world appeared different in those days, weeks, and months following the funeral?

SATURDAY

Morning

List what things count as "work" for you.

List what things feel restful to you (a nap is a given).

Afternoon

When was the last time you drove alone in a car without music?

Sit in silence for five minutes, then write down what bubbles up in your soul. Include the pretty and not-so-pretty things. Invite God to help you explore those things in your soul.

SUNDAY

Morning

Why was Jesus' appearance to Mary Magdalene so significant?

What is the historical Embarrassment Test?

Evening

How was Jesus' resurrected body different from our bodies?

If you could imagine the face of Jesus, what do you think he looks like?

Dale & Jonalyn Fincher

speak and write nationally as a husband-wife team through Soulation (soulation.org), a nonprofit dedicated to helping people become more fully human. Their previous books include *Living with Questions, Ruby Slippers,* and *Coffee Shop Conversations*. Their work has been featured in *Christianity Today, UnChristian, Apologetics for a New Generation, The Washington Post,* and *The Wall Street Journal*. They make their home in Steamboat Springs, Colorado with their son. They love Saturday brunches, classic movies, and hiking in the nearby aspen wood.

Amy Kaneko

is a Hawaii-grown poet who doesn't enjoy long walks on the beach, but loves watching people who do. She is an observer of humans, mother of three, wife of a hunter, and frequenter of used bookstores and farmers markets. Read more of Amy's poetry at amycuriousbird.tumblr.com.

Special thanks to Brandon Hoops, senior editor at
Soulation, who helped compile this book in your hands.
His was the eye for theme and rhythm that suggested
the idea of walking along with Jesus to the cross. Hoops,
you have brought good things to our lives, from heirloom
tomatoes from your grandfather's garden to mailed
articles that you love and know we will enjoy, too (Who
knew Churchill loved to watercolor!). We are grateful for
your love for growth and words on the Soulation writing
team. Hoops, thank you for weaving together these pieces
to make *Long Live the King* possible.

In your debt,
Dale & Jonalyn Fincher

Thank you for sharing the Passion week with us through *Long Live the King*. We love feedback. Please let us know how you enjoyed this book.

To find more thoughtful resources from Soulation, visit soulation.org. New articles and titles are added daily from Dale, Jonalyn, and our writing team.

To purchase *Long Live the King* for a friend, visit amazon.com. To purchase multiple copies for your church or reading group, please contact us for pricing.

Email: mail@soulation.org
Mail: Soulation
        ATTN: Long Live the King
        PO Box 772574
        Steamboat Springs, CO 80487